Ballindalloch Castle
Blair Castle
Dunrobin Castle
Glamis Castle
Scone Palace
Thirlestane Castle and
Traquair

GREAT
HOUSES
OF
SCOTLAND

IAIN GALE · SCOTTISH NATIONAL PORTRAIT GALLERY · EDINBURGH · 2002

Exhibition sponsored by

TURCAN CONNELL
THE PRIVATE CLIENT LAW FIRM

Publication sponsored by

The Kintore Charitable Trust

PREFACE

The Great Houses of Scotland, comprising the seven houses on show here, are all individually owned and open to the public. This group was created in order to benefit from shared knowledge, ideas and collective promotion. The aim is to maintain the uniqueness of each house, while presenting them attractively, with historical accuracy, to a large audience. This exhibition is an enormous boost to those aims and we are unanimous in our enthusiasm for it.

The history of showing off a house and its contents goes back a long way and now more than ever visitors play a vital role in the life of the historic house. It is an integral part of Scotland's history and as history evolves, so too does the house. Today, collectively, these seven houses attract over 445,000 visitors a year. Weddings, banquets, conferences and numerous other events are held in a diverse range of rooms and the grounds play host to a wide assortment of activities. Partnerships are formed with the public, private and charitable sectors, and conservation, presentation and promotion are all important. We acknowledge the help we have received through grant aid and the vital role played by Visit Scotland, formerly the Scottish Tourist Board, in encouraging visitors from abroad.

We enjoy the challenge that our houses offer and are enormously grateful to have the opportunity to take part in this exhibition. We would like to thank James Holloway and the staff of the National Galleries of Scotland for all their efforts in arranging this fascinating exhibition. We would also like to thank Turcan Connell for their generous sponsorship and the Kintore Charitable Trust for sponsoring this publication. Such partnerships have ensured a beautifully presented vignette of our houses, which we hope you will enjoy.

SARAH TROUGHTON
Chairman, The Great Houses of Scotland

FOREWORD

This exhibition and publication celebrate the continuing contribution that Scotland's great houses play in the life of the nation. The seven houses selected for this exhibition form a consortium brought together for the benefit of joint promotion and marketing. The message we present of the inestimable value of the collections held, as it were, in trust for us all, is one that could be repeated many times over in Scotland from Melsetter on Hoy to Lochinch at Stranraer.

Turcan Connell has generously sponsored the exhibition while the publication, which we hope will reach an even wider audience, is financed by the Kintore Charitable Trust. My thanks to them both for their enlightened patronage.

I should also like to thank Sarah Troughton who, as the Chair of The Great Houses of Scotland and the chatelaine of Blair Castle, has been a driving force for the exhibition as has Peter Jarvis, currently the administrator at Thirlestane Castle. The National Galleries of Scotland owes a great debt of gratitude to all the owners who are sharing their family treasures with us. I hope that a visit to the Scottish National Portrait Gallery this winter will prompt further visits to the houses themselves as summer arrives and that we all learn to value the huge contribution Scotland's great houses make to the quality and richness of our lives.

SIR TIMOTHY CLIFFORD
Director-General, National Galleries of Scotland

INTRODUCTION

Scotland is fortunate in the survival of its historic houses and their contents. From glorious palaces like Inveraray and Dunrobin to comfortable lairds' houses such as Craigston and Traquair, Scotland's historic country houses, so many still occupied by the descendants of the men and women who built them, remain not merely treasure chests of art but resources of the greatest value for many aspects of the nation's history.

Britain, fortunately, has largely avoided the political revolutions and devastating wars, which have destroyed so much of value in continental Europe. And Scotland, with its settled, close-knit, often clan-based communities, has not been subjected to the population movements and economic cycles, which in other parts of the British Isles have led to changes of ownership and dispersals.

There was a time when there was real concern that Scotland's houses and their contents were doomed. After the Second World War, with the country still meagerly rationed and highly taxed, the prognosis was bleak indeed. It was then that the National Galleries of Scotland started a programme of recording paintings in private hands, believing that the day was not far off when those collections would be dispersed and the link between the work of art and its original context lost to sight and scholarship for ever. There have been several major dispersals – Cullen and Keir for instance – and many depletions, in particular through the sales of Old Master paintings. But, almost miraculously, most of the great collections have survived the last fifty years, if not intact, at least in reasonably good health. Much of the credit for this is due to the owners themselves who have clung on against reason with stubbornness and determination and by retrenching and diversifying.

Praise is also due to the National Heritage Memorial Fund, the Heritage Lottery Fund and the National Trust for Scotland who have rallied to the defence of houses like Fyvie, Hopetoun, and Newhailes. And it is not just the collections of paintings and sculpture that have survived. Thanks to the assistance of the National Archives of Scotland, family papers, such as those at Blair and Ballindalloch, have been sorted, catalogued and made accessible. The Furniture History Society and the specialist teaching at the University of St Andrews, in particular, have brought a higher level of scholarship to the study of the wonderful collections of native and continental furniture, which enhance so many Scottish properties.

The letter from Rob Roy to William Grant of Ballindalloch – illustrated here – and from George Washington to Grant's brother James are an indication of the richness of the archives in Scotland's country houses. James Grant was engaged in Britain's war against the American colonists when he corresponded with General Washington about safe passage for his men. William Grant was more concerned with the safe passage of his cattle and probably paid protection money to Rob Roy.

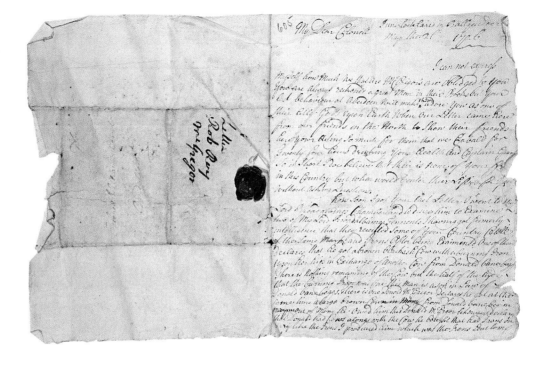

Scotland's landed estates have been in the forefront of agricultural improvement, land reclamation, forestry, livestock breeding, brewing, distilling and sport. They are major employers in parts of the country where employment is often scarce. The first museums of archaeology and natural history in Scotland were displayed in country houses, as were the first portrait galleries and the first collections of Old Master paintings. In recent years, the National Galleries of Scotland have begun to repay this debt by opening outstations at two outstanding country houses: Paxton in the Borders and Duff House in Banff.

Today, government-funded institutions like the National Galleries and the National Museums of Scotland work hand in hand with private custodians. Scotland's country houses contain huge, varied and immensely valuable resources – far too extensive to be taken under the wing of the state. This partnership of state-supported national bodies with enlightened private ownership is the best solution for maintaining Scotland's enviable heritage and for preserving and interpreting it for future generations.

JAMES HOLLOWAY
Director, Scottish National Portrait Gallery

THE GREAT HOUSES OF SCOTLAND

Dunrobin Castle

INVERNESS ● Ballindalloch Castle

ABERDEEN ●

Blair Castle

Glamis Castle

Scone Palace

DUNDEE ●

● GLASGOW

● EDINBURGH

Thirlestane Castle

Traquair

www.great-houses-scotland.co.uk

Thirlestane

Castle

The Maitlands of Thirlestane Castle are a classic example of an important type of country house family. They are the unsung heroes of Scotland's artistic heritage, whose service, over the years, to the development of Scottish art has been as understated – and at times almost unwitting – as it has been vital. At first glance their house and its collections, in the border country of Lauder, might seem to be simply another example of a fine building filled with beautiful things, but a closer acquaintance with their story reveals a deeper significance.

From the beginning, Thirlestane was a castle. Its position in the Leader valley, a mere thirty miles from Edinburgh, made it a prime defence against invasion from the south. In the thirteenth century, William Maitland fought with Robert the Bruce against the English and six generations later, in 1513, his descendant, also called William, died along-side James IV on Flodden field. Their fortress, however, stood firm, unchanged until 1590, when John, 1st Baron Maitland, Lord Chancellor of Scotland to James VI, decided that it was time to rebuild. Still with defence in mind, he constructed a great stone keep. Over the last four centuries the fabric of his building has changed, from defensive stone fortress, to palace, to country house. In its various guises, it has reflected the changing face of the Maitland family and the history and culture of Scotland itself. For the history of any country is no more than many individual stories bound together and by deconstructing one we may gain a unique insight into the other.

In building his keep, Baron Maitland was setting in stone his dynastic ambitions. His portrait, which hangs close to that of his brother in the castle's Panelled Room, shows a man of steely-eyed determination. His brother was no less ambitious and rose to be secretary to Mary, Queen of Scots. The portrait of him by George Jamesone (1589/90–1644) is a posthumous likeness after an earlier work. It is particularly interesting in light of this, that Sir William's nephew, John Maitland, 1st Earl of Lauderdale, who probably commissioned the portrait of his uncle, should have chosen to have his own portrait painted by Adam de Colone (fl. 1622–8), Jamesone's chief rival in Scotland, who had been trained in the Netherlands. Not only is this an important early example of Dutch art in Scotland, but we also know that in 1623 de Colone painted the king. Ally this to the fact that it was Jamesone who painted a series of posthumous portraits of the Scottish kings for the triumphal entry of Charles I into Edinburgh in 1633 and an obvious parallel emerges. De Colone paints both king and earl from life while Jamesone is chosen to paint their ancestors, and thus create a visual genealogy to give tangible form to a lineage. It also reveals a desire on the part of the Maitlands to have their portraits painted by the artists patronised by the monarch and it was this, with its undertones of lofty ambition, which was to be taken to new heights by the following generation.

In 1670, after the ravages of the Civil War, the castle became more of a house, as was the fashion in the Restoration, and a new wing was added. In a reaction against Puritanism, the interiors were embellished with extravagant plasterwork by no less than the king's

own plasterer, George Dunsterfield. His involvement was thanks to the architect, Sir William Bruce, who under John the 2nd earl, later Duke of Lauderdale, was working for the king on similar, timely improvements to the Palace of Holyroodhouse which would reflect the triumphal return of the king and the hopes of a new age. It was Bruce who almost singlehandedly changed the face of architecture in Scotland, by bringing the Renaissance north to temper traditional severity. He brought other things too. Because of him, Lauderdale imported Dutch artists and craftsmen including Jacob de Wet (*c.* 1640–1697) and Jan van Santvoort (1570–1640), both of whom soon secured noble commissions in Scotland. Their legacy to the development of Scottish art is almost incalculable. Naturally, Lauderdale also exploited Bruce's presence for the improvement of his own house and Thirlestane can be seen as a mirror of Holyroodhouse. Lauderdale was both politically and personally ruthless and ambitious. With one hand he imposed the king's stamp on Scottish culture at Holyrood, with the other he ruthlessly crushed the Covenanters. Lauderdale was probably the most powerful man in Scotland. A loyal supporter of Charles I, he had been captured after the battle of Worcester and imprisoned in the Tower of London for nine years, under sentence of death. On his release in 1660, already a confidant of Charles II, he became Secretary of State for Scotland. His portrait by Sir Peter Lely (1618–1680) says it all. He is depicted in a commanding, magisterial pose, clad in state robes and wearing the Order of the Garter, his expression imperious and self-assured. Alas, his triumph was short lived. Charles, persuaded by jealous factions against his grandiosity and apparent greed, dismissed him. He died without male issue in Kent in

LEFT: *John Maitland, Duke of Lauderdale* by Sir Peter Lely

RIGHT: *Sir William Maitland* by George Jamesone

CENTRE: *John Maitland, 1st Earl of Lauderdale* by Adam de Colone

ABOVE: *Charles, 6th Earl of Lauderdale* by William Aikman

BELOW: *Lady Elizabeth Ogilvie, Countess of Lauderdale* by William Aikman

1682 and with him died the dukedom. The earldom though, and Thirlestane, passed to his younger brother and settled into a less regal role, which in a way can be seen to reflect the similar state of the whole of Scotland, gradually sidelined into its eighteenth-century status of 'North Britain'. The castle's history has continued to parallel that of the nation. In 1840, chiefly to meet the needs of the Victorians' penchant for leisure, the house was expanded again. Sensitively remodelled by William Burn and David Bryce, the 1670 version became a fairytale Scots baronial palace that perfectly reflected the spirit of the age and Scotland's place in the affections of Queen Victoria. However, in cultural terms, the house has yet another story to tell. For Lely's painting of the duke is only one from an extensive gallery of family portraits which trace not just the progress of the Maitlands, but also the history of Scottish portraiture. For example, the two portraits by David Scougal (fl. 1661–1677) of the 3rd earl, the duke's successor, and his wife, which were painted before he acceded to the title in 1682, could not be more different in feeling from the painting by Lely. Half-length, intimate and sensitive, they are free of any propagandising effect and emphasise rather the human qualities of the sitters. Scougal was a 'home-grown' artist and it is significant that, disassociated from the world of the London court, the future 3rd earl should have been painted by him while the brash duke chose Lely – principal painter to the king. Here then are two co-existent strata of portraiture prevalent among the Scottish nobility in the second half of the seventeenth century. Early in the next century, however, as Scotland began to establish a strong indigenous portrait tradition, the situation was not quite so clear cut.

It was William Aikman (1682–1731) who painted the 6th earl and his wife. Aikman owed his success as a portraitist not only to his consummate skill, but also to the fact that he came from the same broad social class as his sitters. He was, in effect, painter to the Duke of Argyll whose grandmother, the Duchess of Lauderdale, may have helped Aikman secure this particular commission, highlighting the importance of connections in the development of Scottish portraiture. And it is important too in broader terms. For Aikman was the inheritor of the mantle of Jamesone and Scougal. With a delicate touch he depicts the 6th earl and his wife, imbued with all the confidence of the new age. And in so doing, he continues the artistic tradition which set the tone for the future of Scottish portraiture and the triumph of Allan Ramsay (1713–1784) and Sir Henry Raeburn (1756–1823).

Today, 150 years on, Thirlestane again provides a mirror of the age. Having inherited the castle from his grandmother, the Countess of Lauderdale, in 1972, by 1984, Captain the Hon. Gerald Maitland-Carew was faced with the potential structural collapse of the building. Dry rot was rampant. His solution was the ingenious idea of giving the major part of the castle to a charitable trust, endowed by the National Heritage Memorial Fund. A tremendous success, his scheme – 'the Thirlestane Formula' – has since been much acclaimed and taken up with enthusiasm by other country houses. And so it seems that once again, against the odds, the Maitlands have worked a quiet miracle of sustaining the nation's heritage, while Thirlestane itself promises to survive as a window on Scotland's history and culture.

Glamis

Castle

If you want to bring to mind the image of a Scottish castle just think of Glamis, home of the Earls of Strathmore and Kinghorne – a red sandstone pile of Scots baronial splendour, rising high over the Angus countryside. The name is redolent of Macbeth and other strange and bloody legends, but it is, perhaps, best known as the childhood home of Queen Elizabeth, The Queen Mother. Everything about Glamis speaks of power, history and, importantly, of family, solidity and continuity. The story told by its stones and by the works of art within its walls, is that of the triumph of a dynasty – in building both its house and itself. It is a tale of centuries of good and bad alliances and how such friendships and marriages can make or break a family, just as they can a nation.

The story begins in 1372, when King Robert II granted the thanage of Glamis to Sir John Lyon of Forteviot. Four years later, in 1376, Sir John married the king's daughter, Joanna, and was made Chamberlain of Scotland. It seemed natural to his son, the second Sir John, to consolidate his family's position by constructing a house more serious in aspect than the hunting lodge that had been his childhood home. In 1400, he began work on the east wing of what was to become Glamis. It was the first of many instances at Glamis when the personal aggrandisement of the family, through reward for service or by marriage, would be echoed by physical changes in the house – and vice versa. So it was that, in 1445, ten years after beginning work on the great tower, Patrick Lyon was created 1st Lord Glamis. His great-grandson was not so fortunate. He took as his wife, Janet Douglas, and his family paid dearly for their love. James V, believing himself to have been used by his stepfather, who was a Douglas, took against the clan and began a savage policy of revenge. After the death of her husband, Janet, Lady Glamis, found herself victim of a trumped up charge of witchcraft. She was imprisoned in Edinburgh Castle and burnt to death on Castle Hill. Glamis became forfeit to the crown and it was only after James V's death that the castle was restored to the family – albeit looted of its finest furnishings. Undaunted, in the 1550s the 7th Lord Glamis began a recovery operation and by the end of the century, under his son, the barony was described as having the highest income of any in Scotland. In 1600, Patrick, 9th Lord Glamis, consolidated this fortune and began building the Angle Tower. Once again the advancement of the family mimicked that of the property when, six years later, he was created 1st Earl of Kinghorne by James VI. However, with his son the Glamis fortune would once more fall prey to the consequences of friendship. The 2nd earl, it is said, came to his inheritance the richest peer in the kingdom and left it the poorest. The cause of his impoverishment was his support of the covenanting movement, to which he signed away the family fortune. Siding at first with his friend Montrose, when the latter switched sides, Glamis financed the covenanting army against its erstwhile general. It was an expensive loyalty and in 1670, when the 3rd Earl of Kinghorne took up residence, he inherited not only the castle but the then huge debt of £40,000. The castle's survival today, however, is largely due to his self-discipline and the severe cuts in expenditure that he put in place. Over twenty years the 3rd earl saved and

Seventeenth-century gilded lion

*James Butler,
1st Duke of
Ormonde*
by Sir Godfrey
Kneller

*Patrick Lyon, 3rd Earl of
Strathmore*
by Sir Godfrey Kneller

*John Graham,
Viscount Dundee*
by Sir Peter Lely

remodelled Glamis and in 1677, mirroring this achievement, was created Earl of Strathmore and Kinghorne. His work is everywhere. He altered the focus of the façade, brought a baroque splendour to the main approach and in 1679 constructed the west wing. Inside he built a chapel and, exploiting his connections with the refurbishment of Holyroodhouse taking place at this time, commissioned Charles II's painter, Jacob de Wet, to fill it with magnificent painted panels of religious subjects. The important portrait bust of the earl by Van Santvoort, another of the artists working at Holyroodhouse, also dates from this period. Nowhere is the earl's hand more in evidence than in his refurbishment of the Drawing Room, a 1621 structure, which he described as 'my great hall which is a room that I have ever loved'. It is typical of the sense of continuity at Glamis that the parents of the Queen Mother chose to have Fred Elwell paint their double portrait in this room, beneath the gaze of former earls and echoing the great group portrait, by de Wet, of the 3rd earl and his sons. He is shown in martial pose, clad in the trompe l'oeil body armour of a Roman general. This, of course, is mere fancy. He was no soldier, but a shrewd politician who, through sound judgement and allegiances, ensured the security of his family. This is the man who gazes out from the portrait by Sir Godfrey Kneller (1646/9–1723) – every inch the pragmatist. For, having been a staunch supporter of Charles II, after the Glorious Revolution of 1688 and the advent of King William, Strathmore fared better than his fellow Royalists whose portraits by Kneller and Lely also hang at Glamis – John Graham, Viscount Dundee who fell at Killiecrankie and the Earl of Ormonde, exiled in France. The folly of the covenanting earl was a resounding warning and no sooner had the smoke of the 1689 rebellion cleared than we find Strathmore swearing allegiance to the new succession. And so, despite his armour, de Wet's portrait does not depict him on a battlefield. Strathmore's battles were with debt and the fruit of his victory is to be seen in the distance in the enlarged and resplendent Glamis, looking much as it does today. The 3rd earl had reversed the Strathmores' fortunes. There were still, however, several major dynastic dramas to be played out in the story of both family and building. Despite his grandfather's caution, in 1715 the 5th earl was killed at Sherriffmuir fighting as a Jacobite. It was a salutary lesson, and, while he admired James, the Old Pretender, who stayed at Glamis in 1716 and 'touched' the sick to cure 'the King's evil' in the chapel, his young son the 6th earl did not 'come out' for the Stuarts.

Throughout the eighteenth century the fortunes of the Strathmores did not prosper and to judge by contemporary pictorial evidence, the castle was in poor repair. In 1767, however, the 9th earl took for his wife Eleanor Bowes, daughter of Sir George Bowes of Streatlam Castle in County Durham. She was an heiress and, predictably, new building work followed at Glamis. The west wing was demolished, new kitchens and a billiard room added and the dining room was remodelled. His son the 10th earl, the physical embodiment of the union of the two families did not relent on the building programme. Between 1798 and 1801 he rebuilt the west wing and generally carried on his father's work.

It is hardly surprising that, given the title Lord Bowes and the right to sit in the House of Lords without election, he should have added Bowes to the family surname Lyon. The marriage between the Scots and English families had brought Glamis lasting security. It was to be echoed, on a somewhat grander scale, a century later. It was the name of Bowes-Lyon which on 26 April 1923, Lady Elizabeth, daughter of the 14th Earl and Countess of Strathmore, was to exchange for that of her husband. He was the Duke of York, and as fate would have it, the future King George VI of Great Britain.

Finally, the Bowes-Lyons had made an alliance which would bring not only lasting happiness to the family and to Glamis, but to the entire nation. It was the culmination of a dynastic impetus which had begun some 550 years before when John Lyon had married Princess Joanna. Here at last, in the happy union of two young people, was the closest possible link that could be made between the Anglo-Germanic British Royal family and the blood of Scotland and the Stuarts.

LEFT: *John Bowes, 10th Earl of Strathmore* by Mather Brown

RIGHT: *Queen Elizabeth, The Queen Mother* after Philip de Laszlo

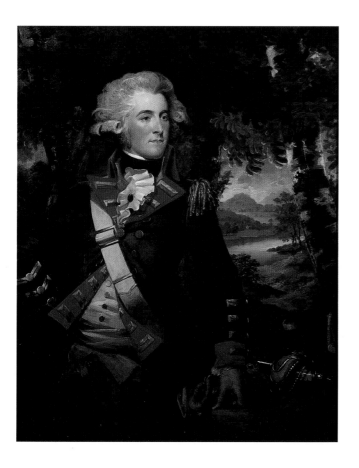

Traquair

A sample of petit point embroidery, c. 1600

The squat stone pillars, each topped with the figure of a bear, support the simple iron gates which are firmly and emphatically shut. The Bear Gates of Traquair have not been opened for the past 250 years. They were closed on an autumn morning in 1745, as the 5th Earl of Traquair waved farewell to his departing prince, Charles Edward Stuart and, according to his oath, they will not open again until the throne of Scotland is held by a Stuart. Many Scottish houses boast links with the Jacobites, but few have so romantic or enduring a tale as Traquair. And the tale has a twist. For Traquair is that rare thing – a house which over the centuries has actually benefited from its loyalty to the Stuart cause and Catholicism. Traquair was originally a royal hunting lodge. The Stuart – now Maxwell Stuart – family moved here in 1478 when it was sold, somewhat unwillingly, by the original owner to James Stuart, son of the king's uncle the Earl of Buchan. Although James Stuart was killed at Flodden alongside his king and his grandson William was captain of Mary, Queen of Scots' bodyguard, it was really only in the seventeenth century that the true depth of Traquair's royalist loyalty became plain.

In 1648 both the 1st and 2nd Earls of Traquair, father and son, were captured by the Parliamentarians after the battle of Preston. The father, John, who in the 1630s had been, as Lord High Treasurer to Charles I, the most powerful man in Scotland, was imprisoned in Warwick Castle. It was only the letters of his wife, Catherine Carnegie, that sustained him while in prison and this testimony of love sets the precedent for what was to become something of a family tradition – the unquestioning and fearless loyalty of a wife to her husband. Despite his wife's tireless support, when John, at the age of fifty-two was released after four years of imprisonment, he was a broken man. Driven to begging in the streets of Edinburgh, he died in poverty in 1659. Five years earlier the second wife of the 2nd earl had brought a further dimension to the complex allegiances of the house, when she introduced Catholicism. From this period dates the secret priests' room designed for the escape of clerics whenever the house was searched – as often it was. It was a trying time and one can imagine the ladies of the house working on their petit point, fearful of the sudden knock at the door, the footsteps in the hall and the arrival of yet another search party hunting down the proscribed priest or the fugitive rebel. Perhaps this is one of the reasons why Traquair today boasts such an impressive collection of embroideries. Previously packed away in trunks and brought out only once a year for inspection, in recent years the collection has become one of the house's most splendid attractions.

The rediscovery of the embroideries might stand as a metaphor for the gradual unfolding of the history of the house and its family. In particular, Traquair's Jacobite connections run deep, continuing research still yields new twists and romantic sub-plots. However, none can be quite so emotive as that of the Nithsdale connection, written about so movingly by Flora Maxwell Stuart. In the dining room at Traquair hang four portraits. Two, by John de Medina the younger (1721–1796), depict the 4th Earl of Traquair and his wife Lady Mary Maxwell, daughter of the staunchly Jacobite Robert Maxwell, 4th Earl of

Nithsdale (the house also boasts fine portraits of the pair by Paton). Beside these hang two more Medina portraits of the 5th Earl of Nithsdale and his wife. The pictures – of Mary, her husband, her brother and his wife – offer a vivid picture of a close-knit group of friends whose story rings through the annals of romantic Jacobitism. It is hardly surprising that Charles, 4th Earl of Traquair should have been involved in the 1715 Jacobite Rising. He was a member of the Jacobite group known as the Braemar Hunting Party, having gone with Nithsdale to meet the Earl of Mar at Braemar on 27 August for a 'hunting match'. Its culmination was the raising of the standard for 'King' James III, but it was a premature action and Traquair was arrested and imprisoned in Edinburgh Castle. His brother-in-law though evaded capture and, with Lords Derwentwater and Kenmure, marched with a Jacobite army into Lancashire. At Preston all were captured and imprisoned, not at Edinburgh, but in the Tower of London. They were sentenced to death. Derwentwater and Kenmure were executed. The story of Nithsdale's escape has become the stuff of legend. It was all thanks to his wife, Winifred Maxwell, who had pleaded with George I for her husband's life, apparently even being dragged on her knees across the floor of the audience chamber on the king's coat tails. But to no avail and so she devised a plan of her own. It was ingenious, if not a little eleventh hour. On the eve of his execution, Winifred visited her husband's cell, accompanied, as was the custom, by two of their female friends. One of them, a Mrs Mills, appeared to the guards to be convulsed with grief, and held a handkerchief to her face. Once in the cell, the women began their work. The other friend, who had dressed in two sets of clothes, removed the outer set and gave these to Mrs Mills, who exchanged them for her own clothes, which she gave to Lord Nithsdale to put on. She was tall and pregnant which was fortunate for, as Medina's portrait shows, Nithsdale was no stripling. His wife then dyed his very masculine heavy eyebrows and rubbed rouge into his cheeks. Meanwhile Mrs Mills, now looking a very different person, left. Shortly afterwards, just as it was getting dark, but before the candles had been lit, Lady Nithsdale and her friend led the grieving 'Mrs Mills' (in fact her husband) from the cell. To judge from the Medina painting, it must have been very dark indeed. Having handed him over to the care of another friend, she returned to 'her husband' in the cell and conducted a one-way conversation with no one, impersonating Nithsdale's voice in reply. Then she too left. Nithsdale was free and was soon reunited with his wife in a tiny garret. There – apparently 'lest their footsteps be heard' – they were 'compelled' to stay in bed together from Thursday to Saturday, before Lord Nithsdale could escape to France. Winifred followed and together they lived out their days in exile at the Stuart court in Rome.

Such uxorial loyalty was to be mirrored in the family thirty years later, during the next great Jacobite rebellion. The urbane 5th Earl of Traquair, a keen art lover who had visited Italy and was responsible for the classical embellishments of much of the house, was equally passionate about his belief in the Stuart cause. The numerous keepsakes and

The Bear Gates

artefacts at Traquair testify to the extent of his faith. The house is filled with Jacobite memorabilia – the mementos which to the loyal supporters of Charles and James were the essence of life. Often given by the prince and his father, they formed tangible, almost mystical links which took on talisman-like properties. They ensured the survival of the faith. And sure enough, when Charles Edward Stuart entered Edinburgh in the autumn of 1745, the Stuarts of Traquair were invited to the Palace of Holyroodhouse. Predictably, having pinned his flag to the mast, Traquair was imprisoned in the Tower of London for two years. His wife, Teresa Conyers refused to leave his side. Probably with the memory of how her husband's family was related to the previous Lady Nithsdale, the governor of the tower, at first, refused her request to lodge with her husband. But Teresa's sheer obstinacy prevailed and stay she did – at considerable family expense – until his release in 1748.

The consistent backing of the wrong party meant that Traquair was ever in need of money and thus it has never suffered from the aggrandising changes which have affected other country houses, but has retained its original charm, modesty and style. Today a more palpable spin-off of the family's allegiance has been the love of the house-visiting public for a good romantic yarn. They have also developed a taste for the famous Jacobite ale which has been brewed at Traquair's own brewery since the 1960s. It might seem a strange paradox that the cause which in so many ways undid Scotland should today benefit the house of some of its most loyal supporters. When the late Peter Maxwell Stuart inherited Traquair in 1962 it had no electric light, and its treasures, along with many of its stories languished under layers of actual and metaphorical dust. Under Peter, the twin assests of its heritage and its brewing were reborn and today, in the care of his widow, Flora, and daughter, Catherine Maxwell Stuart, it welcomes 50,000 visitors a year. Romanticism and real ale make a heady partnership, through which Traquair has managed to preserve its integrity and at the same time ensure its future.

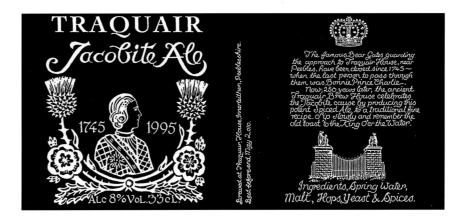

Blair

Castle

Loyalty came naturally to Lord George Murray. It was in his blood. When, in 1745 his prince, Charles Edward Stuart, called for support for a Jacobite rebellion, Lord George, who had already been 'out' thirty years before for Charlie's father James and had been pardoned, again rallied to the cause. Even though he knew the dangers – he had lost many friends to the gallows – still he welcomed the prince, inviting him to stay at his Perthshire home. After the battle of Culloden, George, a hunted fugitive, managed to escape with his life, but would never again see his homeland, as he died in exile in Holland. The story is a familiar one, but in Murray's case it has a greater significance, standing as a metaphor for the leitmotif behind one of Scotland's greatest families and their home, Blair Castle. At its heart Scotland is a country bound by ties of kin and clan, and Blair embodies that allegiance. From the gamekeepers to the people who work in the castle shop, the sense of loyalty at Blair is palpable. It is surely not fanciful to suppose that here is a case of a family trait spreading throughout an estate to the greater 'family' which for some four hundred years it has supported. Blair provides a living example of how in the twenty-first century a country estate can perpetuate and translate, into a contemporary context, virtues forged in another age.

There are two principal sides to Blair today. On the one hand, set in the heart of Scotland's game country, with 140,000 acres, it is managed as a large sporting estate, building on a Victorian obsession to create a thoroughly modern business. On the other it is one of Scotland's leading tourist attractions, with all the concomitant spin-offs which that implies. Both depend on the one thing of which they are also the legacy: a sense of service.

Sitting as it does in the heart of the Highland foothills, Blair has a long tradition of attracting visitors. In 1336 Edward III was a guest and in 1564 Mary, Queen of Scots stayed to hunt deer. Three hundred years later, Queen Victoria spent three weeks holidaying at Blair. Today, while the majority of the visitors are less regal, they are no less important to the house. Opening in 1936, Blair was one of the first country houses in the UK to welcome paying visitors. Last year some 130,000 passed through its gates. They come for a number of reasons: some for a good day out in the country, others to sample how 'the other half live'. Many come to enjoy the extraordinary collection of antiques and works of art assembled by the Murray family over four centuries: Georgian furniture, porcelain, embroidery and paintings. And among those wonders are constant reminders of Blair's abiding twin themes of loyalty and continuity. Perhaps the most obvious evidence of loyalty is the room dedicated to the history of the Atholl Highlanders, the duke's private army and the only one of its kind remaining in Europe. Originally founded during the American Revolution, it never saw active service and was revived only on the orders of Queen Victoria, when it provided a bodyguard for her during her stay at Blair in 1845. Its royal regimental colours, along with the weapons, uniforms and memorabilia housed in its museum are the tangible evidence of the love of a local people for the family who were once their ancestors' masters

An Atholl Highlander with the stag 'Tilt' in the Entrance Hall

ABOVE: *Katherine, 8th Duchess of Atholl*
by Sir James Guthrie

OPPOSITE: *4th Duke of Atholl and his Family*
by David Allan

BELOW: *Death of the Hart in Glen Tilt/*
by Sir Edwin Landseer

and whose name and home still have the power to stir in them some deep-rooted allegiance. Remember, these are no toy soldiers. Ultimately, in theory at least, they can be called on to fight and die, not only for the duke, but also for their monarch and their country. Principally, though, the house resounds to the theme of the field. In almost every room, alongside the visual reminders of the Murrays' own past service of their country – the portraits of dukes in military uniform and that of Katherine Ramsay, 8th Duchess and first Scottish woman Member of Parliament – there is evidence of man's obsession with the chase. Field sports have always been connected with hospitality. To invite a guest – perhaps even a monarch, to shoot, hunt or fish on your land was the ultimate in generosity, demonstrating a friendship or loyalty of the highest order. When Mary, Queen of Scots was treated to a 360 deer day in 1546 it was not merely celebrated as a 'big bag' but as a token of genuine support for her cause. Today's estate supports its sporting activities for other reasons. On one hand they provide a lucrative source of income for the upkeep of the estate, on another they are a valuable source of local employment. At the same time, the use of careful animal conservation and management techniques, ensures that such creatures as the red deer will continue to thrive on Scotland's hills. In 1982, when Iain Murray, the 10th Duke of Atholl was painted dressed in shooting costume with his shotgun and brace of partridge, he was following a family tradition. This is evident in the portrait of the 4th Duke of Atholl and his family by David Allan (1744–1796). The duke is shown as a hunter standing over a dead stag and brandishing a blackcock. Next to him is his keeper, Alexander Crerar, portrayed by Allan with a sensitivity which rivals that of the duke himself. Amongst the paintings at Blair by Sir Edwin Landseer (1802–1873), is one of the young James Murray, brother of the 2nd Lord Glenlyon. In this he is shown playing with a hind, under the watchful eye of the ghillie John MacMillan. Implicit in all of these images is not merely a sense of family, but one of obligation – to a place and to its people. And, importantly, this has always been reciprocal. The 10th Duke of Atholl's portrait was no dry homage to his ancestors. Commissioned by his own tenants, retainers and employees, it was presented to him in honour of his twenty-fifth year as duke. In having him so portrayed they were expressing their thanks for his interest in the estate, his intention to keep it going and his support for the thousands of associated livelihoods it provides. For only by giving of himself could he have the right to expect to be able to command their loyalty. In 1996, Iain, 10th Duke of Atholl died and the title passed to his second cousin once removed, John Murray. Today it is Iain's half-sister Sarah Troughton who, as a trustee of the Blair Charitable Trust, is responsible for the day to day running of the estate and its continuing development. In the last five years Sarah and her architect husband have used their talent and ingenuity to develop the twin paths of tourism and sport with new initiatives of which past generations of Murrays would be proud. At Blair the traditional image of Scotland is no Brigadoon fantasy but a reality, developed naturally over the centuries, whose legacy now provides not only a colourful visitor attraction, but a viable, worthwhile and rewarding way of life.

Scone

Palace

In 1805 the Scottish artist Sir David Wilkie (1785–1841) received an important commission. The 3rd Earl of Mansfield had been much taken by Wilkie's painting *Pitlessie Fair* of the previous year, which his mother, the dowager countess had brought to his attention. It was a ground breaking work – distinctly unheroic in subject matter and yet dealing with a thoroughly human topic that Wilkie managed to imbue with a sense of the extraordinary. It was a celebration of the everyday heroism of the common man. More than this though it had a direct relationship with the theories of the Scottish Enlightenment propounded by the likes of Charles Bell and Thomas Reid – who held that the human face was the mirror of the mind. Mansfield was impressed. And so, in 1806, at the age of only twenty-one, Wilkie fulfilled the commission for the earl in his painting *Village Politicians*, tackling a serious theme with wit and lightness. It is an ostensibly 'low life' subject in which Wilkie declares himself the heir of David Allan, who himself had tackled the subject, by providing the illustrations for the poem which inspired it, Hector Macneill's *Scotland's Skaith or the History of Will and Jean*, published in 1795. The theme of the work is the tragedy of a happy marriage destroyed by the twin evils of drink and radicalism. Specifically it shows Will in a pub seduced from his wife by drink and political passion. Presumably understanding the wishes of his patron, Wilkie builds on the feeling of *Pitlessie Fair*. The individual characters must have appealed to the earl. Everything depends upon expression. And in these expressions, the Enlightenment is palpable. As a result of the work, Wilkie established himself in London as an artist to be taken seriously and this set the tone for his career. As a painting it was mature beyond the artist's years. As an act of patronage it was remarkably enlightened. *Village Politicians* is arguably the most important painting at Scone and, is certainly one of the most significant paintings in the history of Scottish art, its presence there should not surprise us. For Scone Palace is a rare thing. A country house which embodies in its fabric and its contents the tale of a landed family with two distinct yet interlinked attributes – exquisite taste and liberal values. Scone is a living illustration of 400 years of collecting. Here are museum quality pieces of fine French furniture, clocks, sixteenth-century needlework; priceless ivories from Bavaria, Flanders, France and Italy collected by the 4th earl; objets d'art and one of the country's finest porcelain collections. But consider just the Wilkie painting and you will see Scone's true significance, exemplifying the importance of Scotland's country houses and their families as keys to the understanding of the many strands in the development of Scottish art. Scone had always been a seat of enlightened learning. The ancient capital of Pictavia, it became the centre for the Culdees Church and it was here in 838AD that Kenneth Macalpine united Scotland in placing the Stone of Destiny on Moot Hill. Here were crowned all the kings of Scotland including Macbeth and Robert the Bruce. The Scone we see today is largely the creation of the 3rd earl, who had the house rebuilt in the castellated Gothic style by William Atkinson in 1802. But if the 3rd earl was responsible for the palace's outward face, it was the towering personality of his great uncle, William, 1st Earl of Mansfield, who, although he himself spent more time in London, set the tone for its character. If he was absent in his lifetime, at Scone today he is ubiquitous, in portraits by Jacob van Loo, David Martin and Sir Joshua Reynolds (1723–1792). In Reynolds's magisterial 1776 portrait, William, in the robes of the Lord Chief Justice of England, surveys the drawing room with steely-eyed gaze. He was known as 'the greatest lawyer of all time' and certainly, having risen to Lord Chief Justice via Solicitor General and Attorney General, his power was remarkable. Known too as 'silver tongued Murray', he was renowned for his eloquence and persuasive speech making. He was also a key figure in the early years of the movement for the abolition of slavery and it is significant that at the time of the Clearances no one was forced off tenanted land at Scone. That Murray was a man of culture and enlightenment, is quite clearly stated in his portrait by Martin, in which he is depicted seated before a bust of Homer sculpted by Bernini. The Bernini bust is on view in the house beside the painting and close to a marble bust of the earl by Rysbrack. Murray's choice of Homer is significant as enlightened thought at the time stressed that, while Aristotle represented the Greek love of letters, it was Homer who was the real genius, emerging unfettered by the teachings of the establishment. For the earl to embrace the cult of Homer was a far more radical cultural statement than we might today perceive. Here was the lawyer placing his trust not in the letter of the law but on intuitive, natural law. In this the 1st earl clearly presages his great nephew's patronage of the young Wilkie.

William's nephew, David, the 2nd earl was a similarly cultivated man and a vital figure in the history of collecting in Scotland. He was envoy to Dresden and Vienna, and in 1772 was appointed ambassador to the French court, where he remained for some six years. The portraits from Allan Ramsay's studio of George III and Queen Charlotte, which hang at Scone, are a legacy of his tour of duty, many versions having been sent to British embassies in the years following 1760. In Paris, as a friend and confidant of Louis XVI and Marie-Antoinette, David and his wife, Louisa (née Cathcart), enjoyed the lavish artistic and cultural life of Versailles. When they returned to Scotland they brought with them much of the collection which is now at Scone, including many gifts from Marie-Antoinette and Louis XVI and the unique collection of Vernis Martin ware. It is hardly surprising that David should have commissioned such a talent as Johan Zoffany (1733–1810) to paint the breathtaking portrait of his daughter Lady Elizabeth Murray, or that the artist should have painted it as such a homage to *le style Français*. The portrait has another significance, in that Lady Elizabeth is shown with a black girl, Dido Lindsay, the natural daughter of the 1st earl's nephew. The fact that Dido was treated by the earl 'with the same honour as his own nieces' says much for the enlightened character of the Murray family. Once again the ideals of one generation are carried over by another. It was David's wife, as we have seen, who was to introduce their son to Wilkie's work and this is significant. As daughter of the 9th Lord Cathcart, she had already been involved in her own family's important patronage of the work of David Allan, Wilkie's predecessor. Undoubtedly

William, 1st Earl of Mansfield
by Sir Joshua Reynolds

LEFT: *Village Politicians* by Sir David Wilkie

RIGHT: *Lady Elizabeth Murray and Dido Lindsay* by Johan Zoffany

Louisa brought to the family a further dimension on collecting, in particular, through her marriage to a diplomat, strengthening the link between Scottish artists who had already experienced the Grand Tour and their European counterparts. During the time that she and the 2nd earl were at the French court, Allan was in Rome and would certainly have been there at the time of the earl's visit in 1768 when he was painted, like many of his Scottish contemporaries, by Pompeo Batoni. The portrait now hangs in the Ambassador's Room at Scone.

By 1780 Allan was back in Edinburgh, producing portraits of Scotland's great families, including the Cathcarts. It is also significant, given the author of the portrait of Elizabeth Murray, that in these portraits Allan should evince such a tangible debt to Zoffany, admittedly the better draughtsman. Consider too that it was Allan who illustrated Allan Ramsay senior's poem, *The Gentle Shepherd*, published in 1788, which prompted some of his contemporaries to label the poet a 'contemporary Homer'. The connections proliferate across three generations of a family, whose taste in art reveals their abiding character.

Today, while Scone perpetuates much of the sentiment of its previous owners, it is run as a successful business supporting some 150 families, principally in farming and forestry. Working very much in the present, it hosts an annual game fair and central Scotland horse trials. And wherever one looks the contemporary evidence parallels the story played out on its walls – that of an estate supported by and supporting a family of custodians who perhaps more than any other have cause to know the meaning of the term 'enlightened'.

Dunrobin

Castle

As you catch your first breathtaking sight of Dunrobin Castle, towering on its cliff, high above the Dornoch Firth, you would be forgiven for thinking that you had wandered into a Scottish Disneyland. This unlikely edifice, with its crenellations, turrets and tourelles, is the nearest thing we have in Scotland to mad King Ludwig's Bavarian Schloss Neuschwanstein. Yet, for all its owners' lofty status, Dunrobin was the product not of megalomania but careful, considered thought. It stands as the physical embodiment of a family's desire to imprint the values of the early modern world on a country reluctant to accept them and as a monument to both the dangers and the benefits of passionate enthusiasms.

The Dunrobin to which Elizabeth Gordon brought her husband after their wedding in 1785 was a very different place. The draughty, baronial castle was an unlikely home perhaps for a woman considered one of the beauties of her age. A woman who had turned even Lord Byron's head. Her portrait by Sir Thomas Lawrence shows her to be the embodiment of the Regency belle – every inch a Jane Austen heroine – if of somewhat grander birth. In 1766, on the death of her father the 18th earl, and as a result of the ruling of the expensive Sutherland Peerage Case, the title passed to the female line and Elizabeth became Countess of Sutherland. The man she took for her husband could hardly match her for looks. George Granville Leveson-Gower, 2nd Marquis of Stafford, 3rd Earl Gower, Viscount Trentham, 4th Lord Gower of Stittenham was not a particularly attractive man. His portrait by Owen with his stern face and aquiline nose suggests a clearly determined character. His letters, however, reveal a quiet, bookish man. The marriage of the Gordons and the Leveson-Gowers was a significant alliance of one of the greatest Highland estates to considerable lands in England – at Trentham in Staffordshire and Lilleshall in Shropshire – and it made George one of the most notable men in Britain. But George was cursed with one significant trait. He was a do-gooder. All he wanted to do was help. In particular, he wanted to bring the values of the nascent industrial and social revolutions to a Britain whose countryside he saw as being sunk in the Dark Ages. Thus, he undertook a programme of 'improvement'. His English estates benefited from new roads and new bridges. In Scotland, though, he came unstuck. George did not understand the Highlands. He was essentially English in temperament and outlook and considered the place savage and backward. His wife, rooted more in the life of the London court than her ancestral home, shared his views. But George had married into a Highland family and with wealth came a responsibility to his tenantry. Unfortunately for them, George believed in 'necessary evils'. If the few must suffer to ensure the future of their descendants, then so be it. For advice about land reform he consulted not a highlander but James Loch, an Edinburgh man with an accountant's mind and a heart of granite. The resulting 'improvements', a significant episode of the Highland Clearances, caused untold suffering to more than 5,000 people. For decades George was castigated as an 'evil man', but now he is recognised for his misguided philanthropy. Old wounds still smart, however, and it might seem ironic to many today that he considered himself a Liberal and that he should actually have been

A crocodile from the natural history collection at Dunrobin

created 1st Duke of Sutherland as reward for his support for the 1832 Reform Bill. He died six months later, and was succeeded by his son, who brought a very different character to Dunrobin.

This was the castle's golden age. Physically unlike the first duke, his son, also called George, was very different in temperament. He was aged forty-seven when he inherited the title, with a wife twenty years his junior and both were, in their own way, to contribute to the story of Dunrobin, its architecture and its ethos. Duchess Harriet was, as her mother-in-law had been, a beauty. She was also a wit and a formidable woman. She was by birth a Carlisle Howard and her marriage, another society alliance probably engineered by her mother-in-law, cemented the Anglo-Scottish dukedom to another of the most prestigious of English families in which the names of Carlisle, Devonshire, Marlborough and Bedford are writ large. Unsurprisingly, Harriet was Mistress of the Robes to Queen Victoria. And, more importantly, she was the queen's personal confidante. Harriet was nothing if not shrewd. At court in London she behaved, it was said 'like a head housemaid', being careful not to outshine the queen. However, when Queen Victoria visited her on her home ground, it was another matter. 'I come from my house', said the courteous queen, 'to your palace'. Her words were no exaggeration. The 2nd duke did not share his father's enthusiasm for politics and was much more interested in his houses. In 1844 he commissioned Sir Charles Barry to transform Dunrobin into a house worthy of his family. Barry, the architect of the Houses of Parliament, turned the old castle into a dream of the Loire valley – a Scottish Chenonceaux. As can be seen in James Giles's oil painting (before the fire of 1915 and subsequent, sympathetic restoration by the architect, Sir Robert Lorimer), Barry's new Dunrobin was a vast French palace of fairytale splendour. It is probable that Queen Victoria's high opinion of Dunrobin was influential in the architectural makeover of Balmoral, bought in 1848 and transformed in the 1850s by Prince Albert. It is also likely that the queen's empathy with the taste of the Sutherlands, resulted in her own Italianate Osborne House on the Isle of Wight being modelled in the style of Trentham Hall. For Sutherland had already commissioned Barry to remodel Trentham in a fashionably Italianate manner. No sooner had the architect completed Dunrobin, than Sutherland set him to work on designing another pseudo-Renaissance palace, whose name was to carry for another hundred years into the annals of high society – Cliveden. It was an indication of Duchess Harriet's influence over her husband that Cliveden was modelled on the Villa Albano in Rome. The Sutherlands' patronage of Barry also extended to Stafford House, their London home (now Lancaster House), originally built for the Duke of York, son of George III. Of all their houses, it was Stafford House which, more than any other, became celebrated as a gathering place for society. And under Harriet's influence, it also emerged as a centre of 'reform'. For hand in hand with the zest for architectural improvement, went that of social innovation. The 2nd duke

ABOVE: *Harriet, Duchess of Sutherland and Lady Elizabeth* by Sir Thomas Lawrence

OPPOSITE ABOVE: *Spring (Lady Constance)* by Sir Edwin Landseer

OPPOSITE BELOW: *Autumn (Lady Evelyn)* by Sir Edwin Landseer

was not, thankfully, quite so zealous as his father. While he allowed his agents to carry on his father's work, he was inclined to more effective acts of generosity, remitting rent arrears on his mother's death and in the year of the Highland famine, spending some £78,000 of his own money to relieve the suffering. Harriet, in her own reforming passions, was no less fervent and was a genuine, concerned champion of the oppressed. By the middle of the century, at her personal invitation, Lord Shaftesbury had made Stafford House the venue for his important reform meetings. In March 1853, Harriet herself held a meeting there of some forty society ladies who resolved to send a petition signed by several thousand like-minded women calling for the abolition of slavery, to one Harriet Beecher Stowe, author of *Uncle Tom's Cabin*. The alliances and promises made during daytime meetings at Stafford House were compounded by friendships cemented at its celebrated evening soirées. Lami's watercolour of the house showing Queen Victoria arriving for a reception is a revealing testimony to the power and influence of the Sutherlands – culturally, socially and politically. The Sutherlands, assiduous in cultivating their circle of friends, were no less passionate in other fields of 'collecting'. Queen Victoria had been impressed not only by the architecture of Dunrobin but also by its magnificent paintings, in particular, the works by Sir Edwin Landseer. The collection had principally been amassed by the 1st duke. In one year alone, he had spent £30,000 on paintings for Dunrobin. But the house held (and holds) many other treasures and surprises – not least in its museum. It was the 3rd duke's idea to create a home for various objects of interest that the family had amassed and which he felt might be of value to posterity. With the generations it grew reflecting the fashion of the time, be it the taste of the hunter for big game trophies, or that of the amateur naturalist for stuffed birds. One of its most interesting and important aspects is its extraordinary collection of Pictish remains, in particular, the standing stones carved with depictions of beasts, and artefacts which trace the history of Sutherland back into unrecorded time. It is significant that a family whose blood was by the Victorian era so undeniably cosmopolitan, should have taken such an interest in the past – seeking to find for itself a tangible connection with the land and all that it once held – from the intricately carved bog oak of the sgian-dubhs of past generations, to the stuffed stags and birds which once roamed the hills. The Sutherlands' private museum holds another level of meaning which in a way sums up this extraordinary place. To modern eyes this passion for taxidermy might seem grizzly, cruel and mawkish but to its original curators, the museum was a thing of wonder – a source of inspiration and knowledge. And both in the museum and in the manners and mores of its owners, Dunrobin reminds us that the past is a foreign country. A country we cannot judge by the values of our own age. It has many lessons for us and many warnings, but we must always take the past on its own terms.

Ballindalloch

Castle

Ask the owner of any great house and they will tell you that inheriting is the easy part, it is hanging on to the place that is hard. You have to work at it. Successfully perpetuating a house and its contents for future generations is all about security. In its oldest manifestation of course this took the very literal form of repelling the invader, consequently, castles had a clearly defined purpose. Ballindalloch Castle, nestling in the Spey valley, was originally built as a defence sometime in the sixteenth century. The Grant family acquired the land in 1532 but did not occupy the site until 1546. A branch of the family has been here ever since, sustained by a winning combination of three things – tenacity, patience and a penchant for strategic planning.

The original castle of Ballindalloch was a tower house – that uniquely Scottish creation – tall, imposing and strong enough to stand up to both the Highland winds and the best efforts of any potential adversary. With passing generations, the threat to the future security of the Grants became less militaristic and more economic. In the early eighteenth century, it was not force of arms that drove the descendants of Patrick Grant from his castle, but financial necessity. However, by selling it to a cousin, the family could take consolation in the fact that it remained a Grant house.

The castle, originally built to the classic z-plan, ideal for the enfilading fire which would break up any attack, was remodelled in the 1850s as a purely decorative fortification with a plethora of the rounded turrets and gentle period detailing of the Scots Baronial style. The starkness of the original sixteenth-century tower house was removed and in its place arose the sort of comfortable country house typified by the royal benchmark of Balmoral. Today, in the wake of further sensitive refurbishments carried out in the 1960s by the parents of the present owner, the overwhelming impression as you wander through Ballindalloch remains one of being in a genteel and welcoming Victorian country house. That the castle functions on a domestic scale is only because of its subsequent alterations. With a little imagination, it is possible to strip away the panelling and plasterwork and understand the scale of the original. Such leaps in time are manifest not only in the building but also in its parkland. Here is a herd of cattle. Deep black in colour, they seem quite different from the commonplace cow, and they are. These are no mere cattle but Balindalloch's unique, prize-winning Aberdeen Angus, the oldest Scottish herd in continuous existence. The rural scene in the grounds at Ballindalloch is precisely that which would have been found here in 1860 when this world-famous herd of black hornless cattle was established by Sir George Macpherson-Grant, great-grandfather of the present lady laird of Ballindalloch, Clare Macpherson-Grant Russell. Over the years, great care has been taken to ensure the survival of the breed and there are parallels to be found in the history of the family and, in particular, the stories of two men.

The Grant cousins who took over the house in 1711 came from a military family as a look at the line of succession shows: William Grant, colonel d. 1733; Alexander Grant, captain, d. 1751; William Grant, major, c. 1770; James Grant, general d. 1806. And we should pause here. For the general was no ordinary soldier. That he was born to the colours is evident in Richard Waitt's portrait of him as a child. Dressed in military uniform, here is the second son of the house, bound, not to inherit the estate, but to serve in the army. James Grant entered the British army a young man and retired from it after sixty years continuous service. The passage of the years is obvious in a later portrait attributed to Staveley. The general is shown as a wealthy and successful man – a soldier, politician, landowner, businessman and epicure. His story is told in a fascinating and extensive archive of personal papers – so significant that they are currently being put on microfilm by the US Library of Congress. From them we learn how the impoverished army officer, compelled to borrow money to purchase his way up the ladder of commissions, prospered through a combination of war, politics and his own shrewd strategy.

Grant first distinguished himself in the Seven Years' War, 1756–63, waged throughout the colonies. He was a pragmatist, described by his current chronicler Dr Robert Clyde as being 'at the hawkish end of the British army'. It seems curious then that, given the post-war task of rooting out the Cherokee, he did not opt for wholesale massacre, but instead burnt their crops, earning for himself the Indian nickname 'Corn-puller'. For his troubles, Grant was rewarded with the governorship of Florida and, over the next decade, built up a prosperous business in the colony by establishing a large and profitable plantation for the growing of indigo. Following his brothers' death with no issue, the general inherited Ballindalloch in 1770 and quickly began to use his new found wealth to enrich his house by adding north and south wings. On the outbreak of the War of Independence, Grant rejoined the colours and travelled to fight the colonists. While he was away in the northern colonies, his plantations still prospered, making money for him while he was in the thick of the fighting. At the end of the American war, Grant was able to return to Ballindalloch a rich man, ensuring the survival of the estate. A giant of a man and a favourite of George III, he brought with him a reputation for the good life. Fortunately though, this did not extend to the gaming tables of London which impoverished the estates of so many of his landed contemporaries. The general's chief vice was for the table. During the war, even as the bullets had flown, Grant had been at his table in his tent, dining off porcelain and silver. Not least among the improvements he made to Ballindalloch was to have a wing built to house his favourite chef, a French-speaking African slave.

Such was the financial security that the general brought to Ballindalloch, that his grand-nephew, George Macpherson of Invereshie, who had inherited the property from his uncle in 1806, was honoured in 1838 by being created a baronet. George further consolidated the castle's future by bringing together the Macphersons and the Grants, styling himself Sir George Macpherson-Grant, 1st Baronet of Ballindalloch. The parallel phenomena of duty to both the nation and the house continued with the 2nd baronet, Sir John Macpherson-Grant who, while serving as a diplomat – notably in Lisbon – amassed

General James Grant as a Young Boy
by Richard Waitt

a good collection of seventeenth-century Spanish paintings. He was also responsible for the Victorian alterations to the house. But it was Sir John's son George who gave Ballindalloch its modern day character with the creation of the now world-famous herd of Aberdeen Angus cattle. David Steell's evocative studies of the early stars of the herd are a homage to the creatures which were, and are still today, an important part of the life-blood of Ballindalloch. To call Sir George's introduction of cattle to the estate masterly would be an understatement. In addition to creating a herd that would remain in demand and would win for the family trophy after trophy, he saw another dimension. His timing was perfect. For cattle could be 'finished off' on grass, thus allowing the oats and barley grown at Ballindalloch to be sold to a prospering industry then only recently legalised – the local whisky houses of such names as Glenfarclas and Glenlivet. Once again, a laird of Ballindalloch had looked beyond the obvious to find a way of making his money work and his house secure.

Ballindalloch Ericas by David Steell

In the 1970s, a new generation of Macpherson-Grants arrived at the castle, when the current lady laird brought her husband, Oliver Russell, to live at her ancestral home. Faced with the typical financial problems associated with the upkeep of a Highland estate, they were confronted by the common solution of selling off their land piecemeal. However, Russell, as a banker, was a natural planner – a strategist who realised the long-term folly of disposing of such assets. Instead they devised a strategy to provide the income to make the estate work. It was a bold move, but one thoroughly in keeping with the spirit of the place. Today, the laird and her husband run the castle as a team, 'he looks at the overall bigger picture', she says, 'and I put it into practice and take care of the minutiae.' A cherished family home, Ballindalloch also functions as a successful business and the various financial strategies put in place over past decades look set to ensure its continued survival. Recent initiatives include the expansion of the castle's role as a venue for corporate hospitality and the construction of a new golf course. What is significant is that none of this is change for its own sake. It is the sympathetic development of a Highland estate in tune with modern times: the use of innovation and forward planning to perpetuate a unique part of the heritage of a family and a nation. The general and Sir George would quite understand.

Published by the Trustees of the National Galleries of Scotland to
accompany the exhibition *Great Houses of Scotland* held at the Scottish
National Portrait Gallery, Edinburgh from 25 January to 21 April 2002.

ISBN 1 903278 26 0

Designed and typeset in Throhand and Minion by Dalrymple
Printed by BAS Printers, Over Wallop

Cover illustration: letter from Rob Roy to William Grant
of Ballindalloch, from the archives at Ballindalloch Castle.
Photo: Antonia Reeve